Contents

What are **puppets?**

Puppets are toys that can be made to move. They are moved in different ways.

This puppet moves when you pull on its strings.

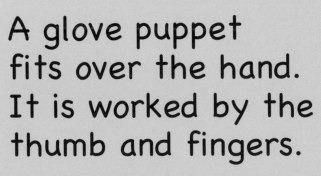

A glove puppet fits over the hand. It is worked by the thumb and fingers.

Ways into Technology

Puppets

Written by Claire Llewellyn

W
FRANKLIN WATTS
LONDON • SYDNEY

First published in 2008 by Franklin Watts
338 Euston Road
London NW1 3BH

Franklin Watts Australia
Level 17/207 Kent Street
Sydney NSW 2000

Copyright © Franklin Watts 2008

Editor: Julia Bird
Art director: Jonathan Hair
Design: Shobha Mucha
Photography: Paul Bricknell
Consultant: Pam Bolton, design and technology advisor

A CIP catalogue record for this book
is available from the British Library

ISBN 978 0 7496 8080 0

Dewey Classification 688.7'224

Printed in China

Every attempt has been made to clear copyright.
Should there be any inadvertent omission please
apply to the publisher for rectification.

With thanks to our models: Kalem Patel, Kheilah
Viljoen, Lucas Dyson-Diaz, Sacha Seresin and Sophie
Gunn. Thanks also to Lesley Butler, Puppet Planet,
for the loan of puppets on pp.6, 7, 8, 10, 26 and 27.

Franklin Watts is a division of Hachette Children's
Books, an Hachette Livre UK company.

This puppet is worked by sticks called rods.

These are finger puppets.

How do you think they move?

 Puppet materials

Puppets can be made of many different materials.

This puppet is made of paper.

Kheilah's puppet is made of cloth. It has sparkly stars and beads.

This puppet is
made of wood.
Its face and body
have been painted.

Look at these materials.
How could you use them
to make a puppet?

pom poms

felt pieces

feathers

wool

wiggly
eyes

sequins

Looking at **characters**

In a puppet show, the puppets are used to tell a story. Each puppet plays a different character.

This puppet is a pirate. He has a patch and a hook.

This puppet is a good fairy. She looks very kind.

Kheilah is making a puppet of a man using a paper plate and a lolly stick.

She wants to make him look angry.

Hair stands on end

Frown

Eyebrows are big and low over the eyes

Mouth is open, showing big teeth

Staring eyes

How could she make the puppet look scared?

A **pencil** puppet

Kalem is making a pencil puppet.

1 He draws a chicken's head on a piece of card.

Then he carefully cuts it out. He has made a template.

2 He pins the template to two pieces of yellow cloth. He cuts around it. Now he has two heads that look the same.

12

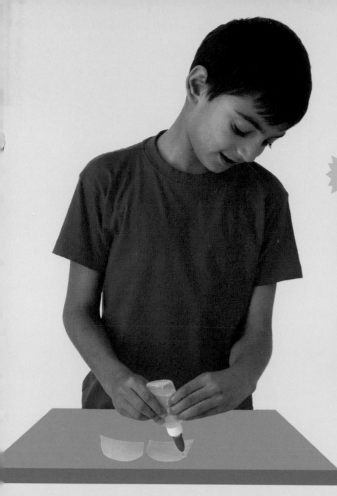

3 He glues around the edge of one head, leaving the neck free.

He presses the other head on top.

4 He decorates the puppet with some red felt and two wiggly eyes and puts it on a pencil.

How else could Kalem have joined the two heads together?

Finger puppets

Kheilah wants to make two finger puppets for her friend Sacha.

1 First, she rolls some paper around her finger to see what size the puppets need to be.

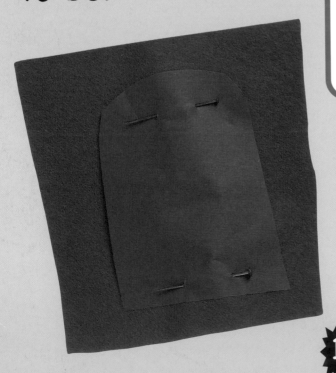

Toolbox
- Scissors • Paper • Felt
- Stapler • Glue • Wiggly eyes

2 She cuts the paper to the right size. Then she pins it to two pieces of felt and cuts around it.

3 She staples the two pieces of felt together, leaving a gap for her finger. She decorates her puppets with pieces of pink felt and wiggly eyes.

When Kheilah has finished her finger puppets, she gives them to her friend.

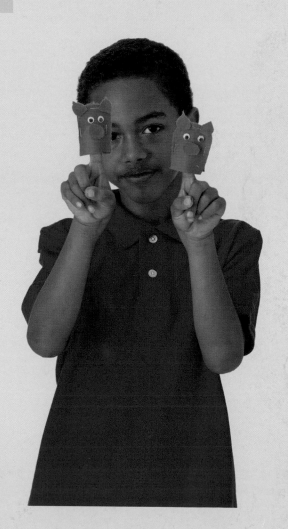

Safety note:
Take care with staplers.
They are very sharp.

A **cardboard** puppet

Lucas has found a template of an alien puppet. It has four pieces.

He copies the pieces onto card. Then he cuts them out.

Toolbox
- Template • Pens • Thread
- Scissors • Hole punch
- Split pins • Lolly stick

Lucas makes holes in the puppet's joints using a hole punch.

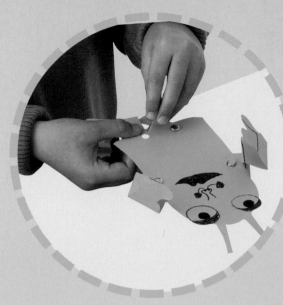

He uses split pins to join the puppet together.

Lucas punches a hole at the top of the puppet. He puts thread through the hole, then tapes it to a lolly stick.

Now he can make the puppet move!

Why don't you try making a puppet from a template?

Planning a **glove** puppet

Sophie is planning a puppet show of Goldilocks and the Three Bears.

Sophie is making a bear puppet. She plans the puppet on a piece of paper.

Beige felt for ears

Black felt for eyes

Red felt for mouth

Next, she draws around her hand to see how big the puppet needs to be.

Now she draws the shape of the puppet around her hand to make a template. She cuts it out.

Toolbox
- Pens
- Scissors
- Paper

What does Sophie do with the template next? Turn the page to find out.

Cutting the puppet

Sophie pins her puppet template to two pieces of cloth. Then she carefully cuts around it.

Now she has two puppet shapes. She needs to join them together.

Can you think of some different ways she could do this?

Sophie decides to sew her puppet. Sewing is easy and makes the puppet very strong.

She gets out the sewing tools.

What do each of the tools do?

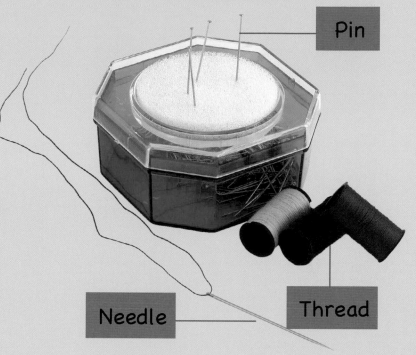

Pin

Needle

Thread

Toolbox
- Pins
- Pincushion
- Needle
- Thread

Why not make and sew your own glove puppet?

How will you join the pieces?

Sewing the puppet

Sophie decides to sew her puppet together to make it strong.

Sophie takes a needle and thread. She ties a knot at one end of the thread.

Now she is ready to start sewing!

Sophie sews carefully all around the edge of the puppet. She makes sure she leaves a gap for her hand.

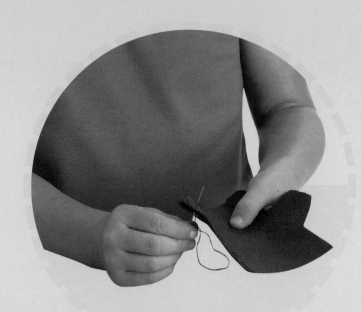

At the end, she does two stitches on top of each other. Then she cuts the thread.

Try sewing your own puppet. How can you make your stitches good and strong?

Finishing off

Sophie decorates her puppet by gluing on some pieces of felt to give it eyes, paws, ears, a nose and a mouth.

> It fits my hand.

> I like the felt. It feels soft.

> I don't like the colour. I'll use red next time.

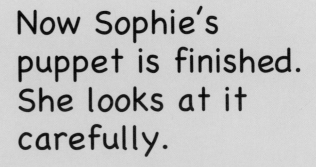

Now Sophie's puppet is finished. She looks at it carefully.

24

What do you think of your puppet?

Would you change anything about it?

I think I'll draw the beard next time.

My alien's great!

Maybe I should use glue instead of staples.

25

Puppets picture quiz

Look at the puppets on this page. How do you make them move?

Now look at some other puppets. Decide what materials each puppet is made from. Make a record of your results on a table like this.

	Wood	Material Paper	Cloth	Card	How does it move?
				✓	String
			✓		Hand
			✓		Fingers
	✓				Rods
				✓	Lolly stick
			✓		Hand

Useful words

character – a person in a story.

cloth – a fabric made from wool, cotton or other sort of fibre.

decorate – to add extra things like feathers or sequins to improve the look of the puppet.

felt – a kind of cloth.

hole punch – a tool for punching holes into paper and other materials.

knot – a little lump on the end of a piece of thread. It is made by tying the ends together.

materials – things like paper, wood and cloth which can be used to make puppets and many other things.

needle – a long metal pin with a small hole. It is used to pull thread when sewing.

pin – a short sharp piece of metal that is used to join cloth or paper together.

pincushion – a small cushion to stick pins and needles into until they are needed.

sequin – a small flat shiny piece of plastic that we sew onto cloth to decorate it.

sew – to join cloth by making stitches with a needle and thread.

split pin – a pin with a stem that is split into two parts.

stapler – a tool for punching staples into paper and other materials.

template – something that is used as a guide for cutting cloth or other material.

thread – a very fine cord that is used for sewing.

Some answers

Here are some answers to the questions we have asked in this book. Don't worry if you had some different answers to ours; you may be right, too. Talk through your answers with other people and see if you can explain why they are right.

page 7   Finger puppets move when you wiggle your fingers.

page 9   The wool could be used to make hair or a beard. Wiggly beads could be used to make eyes. The sequins could be used to decorate a crown. Feathers could be used on a puppet of a bird or for hair. Felt shapes can be used to make little extras like a nose, ears and paws. Pom-poms could be used to make a nose or for clothes decorations.

page 11   Kheilah could make the puppet look scared by lifting the eyebrows, making the eyes larger, and drawing a wiggly mouth.

page 13   Kalem could have stapled or sewn the heads together.

page 20   Sophie could staple them, glue them or sew them together.

page 21   Pins are used to hold two pieces of cloth together. The needle and thread are used to stitch the cloth together. The pincushion holds pins and needles safely until they are ready to use.

Page 23   You can make stitches strong by making them small and keeping them close together.

Index

About this book

Ways into Technology is designed to encourage children to begin to think about how things are designed and made in the world around us.
Here are some pointers to gain maximum use from **Puppets**.

Working though this book will introduce the basic concepts about puppets and how they are designed and made, and also some of the vocabulary associated with them (for example, character, decorate, materials, template). This will prepare the child for more formal work in Design and Technology later in the school curriculum.

As you read through the book with children, ask them to point to each puppet and say what kind of character it depicts, what it is made of and how it moves. Discuss with children which tools were used to make it.

On pages 7, 9, 11, 13, 20, 21 and 23, readers are invited to answer a question or suggest an alternative way of doing something. Ensure that you discuss any answer they give in some depth before moving on. Perhaps you could set up other scenarios for the children to predict and discuss possible outcomes. For example, on page 9 you could find alternative materials from those in the photo. On page 11, you could try drawing faces to show different emotions.

Pages 26-27 are an opportunity to revisit material in the book. Make sure that children are familiar with the names for all the different kinds of puppets, tools, materials and actions used in the book.